Tory Shepherd is a senior News Corp columnist and *The Advertiser*'s state editor. She spent several years in the Canberra Press Gallery and contributes to *The Project*, *The Drum*, *Sunrise*, *Today* and ABC radio.

T0359825

Writers in the *On Series*

Tory Shepherd

On Freedom

hachette
AUSTRALIA

Published in Australia and New Zealand in 2020
by Hachette Australia
(an imprint of Hachette Australia Pty Limited)
Level 17, 207 Kent Street, Sydney NSW 2000
www.hachette.com.au

First published in 2019 by Melbourne University Publishing

10 9 8 7 6 5 4 3 2 1

A catalogue record for this book is available from the National Library of Australia

ISBN: 978 0 7336 4427 6 (paperback)

Original cover concept by Nada Backovic Design
Text design by Alice Graphics
Author photograph courtesy of News Corp
Typeset by Typeskill
Printed and bound in Australia by McPherson's Printing Group

To all the well-meaning numpties who keep asking women when they're going to have a kid, or why they're not, or when the next one's coming, or why they haven't tried vaginal steaming. I hope you read this, and stop.

In the beginning

Whenever they went, 'What? No children?
Well, you'd better get on with it, old girl,'
I'd say 'No! Fuck off!'
Actor Helen Mirren, who later confessed she
had a fleeting regret about not having kids

Mum once (jokingly, I think) threatened to replace my contraceptives with sugar pills. She was keen for grandkids, while I had no instinct, no urge, no drive to reproduce. It was swiftly made clear to me by the external world that was an absence, an abnormality. The very sentence feels like a staccato I've repeated all my life. No instinct, no urge, no drive. Followed by a sometimes harrowing guilt at not being a full woman. And an anxiety that I was deficient.

Years later (more seriously) Mum told me that she was glad she did not have the freedom my generation has to choose children. She saw child-choice freedom as a burden.

Babies or no babies at all or how many babies and when? With whom and why? If it's possible to get choice fatigue in the olive oil aisle at the supermarket, how much harder is choosing what kind of family to have? Especially when we're bombarded with images of the ideal family—advertisers baulk at depicting a household of one.

My fiercely independent mother was the bringer of the bacon as well as the bearer of the three of us in the seventies. Sure, women had the Pill then. And she was in touch with her bohemian self: she hitch-hiked through Europe for years, doing timeshare on beds in London, whitewashing Greek villas and sleeping on the beach. But once she came back to Adelaide and got married, it was close to unthinkable to pick a childfree path.

When my mother finally realised that I was not for turning, that I would not choose motherhood, she confessed she couldn't be sure what she would have done in the same situation. She didn't have the childlust some women had, and she had a fulfilling career. She can see now that in a different century with different norms, she would have been torn. To kid or not to kid. How many, when.

Don't get me wrong, Mum's chuffed she had us; particularly because the three of us moved out of home at a reasonable age and we're more or less functional. (More or less.) She never had to sit through her mid-thirties wondering *if* she should have kids, while clocks ticked and biddies tutted and careers beckoned. Freedom of choice is *hard*, and she didn't have to face that. She did the done thing.

With all this freedom, why is having children (or not) more complicated than ever? It turns out freedom of choice can be a burden. Having just the childbearing path in front of you would be so simple. Now there are so many paths diverging in the woods, it's much harder to pick which one to travel by.

Women in Australia and most of the developed world are increasingly having fewer kids, having them later, or not having them at all. The decision not to have children isn't made in a vacuum and is often chosen in the face of stigma and discrimination, with the extended families of these women sometimes left feeling confused and betrayed by the choice. Not to mention the complete strangers, who frequently act as though they're confused and betrayed as well.

There lingers a sense that the childless-by-choice woman is unnatural, barren, weird. Selfish, career-obsessed, cat-loving. A bit witchy.

Meanwhile, women who have chosen to be parents are under more pressure than ever to be perfect. To not just 'have it all'—a career and kids and a partner—but to live up to the unrealistic expectations of the filtered world of social media. One in which you bake an *Australian Women's Weekly* birthday cake before donning sexy lingerie to show off your mum bod, before getting up at 5 a.m. the next day to meditate before running a sprightly 10 kilometres and planking till you drop, then cooking an Insta-worthy meal before applying just the right hydrating cream and uploading a sleep app so you can do it all again tomorrow. It is mind-deadeningly facile to constantly repeat all that, but many women feel overwhelmed by an endless stream of boxes they feel the need to tick daily.

It was easier, back in my mum's day. You got married, had kids. We were latch-key kids, getting on the bus with backpacks as big as our torsos, riding around without seatbelts, being dragged to goonbag-fuelled dinner parties where we'd sneak sips and after-dinner mints and go to sleep on beds piled with jackets that smelled like cigarettes. Imagine a modern mother letting any of that happen.

There have always been mainstream expectations of motherhood, and mainstream suspicions that fall on those who don't join the club, even as the statistics show a significant shift of women saying no to children. An untold number of articles has been written over the years lamenting the fact that US actor Jennifer Aniston hasn't had kids. Though she has repeatedly asserted she's totally fine about it, glossy-magazine readers with glassy eyes can't imagine that she's not devastated she didn't cook up a kid with former husband Brad Pitt. Readers spend hours discussing online the plight of 'Sad Jen', the barren, weepy superstar.

And many of us will never forget when former Liberal senator Bill Heffernan said Julia Gillard was not fit for leadership because she was 'deliberately barren'. The phrase conjured the archetypal image of the childless woman as embittered and cold, a non-woman because she had not had life in her womb. Before that, and before she became the new Labor leader, Ms Gillard had been photographed at home in her humble retro kitchen. An empty bowl sat on the table.

That's what people noticed. Not the profile of a woman destined for greatness, but her kitchen's lack of fruitful domesticity. The metaphor of the empty fruit bowl haunted our first female prime minister throughout her tenure.

More recently, Pope Francis, whom many still consider a moral authority despite all the child sex abuse cover-ups within his church, declared voluntary childlessness 'selfish'. 'A society with a greedy generation, that doesn't want to surround itself with children, that considers them above all worrisome, a weight, a risk, is a depressed society. The choice to not have children is selfish,' the pontiff said.

He and his ilk can pontificate all they want; more women are staying childless and that won't be fixed by appeals to God or country. The Australian Bureau of Statistics charts a steady decline in the number of families living with children—at one point they pre-dicted that the number of couple families living without children would outstrip those with children in another decade.

The Australian fertility rate—the average number of children born per woman—in 2017 was 1.74. That's not enough to 'replace' the present population. A comprehensive, world-first study published in *The Lancet* recently looked at childbirth in 195 countries from 1950 to 2017. It found fertility rates are declining in countries where women have more freedom due to increased education, better access to contraception, and lower infant mortality rates (an effect of better support and healthcare). These very personal and complicated choices being made (mostly) by women are already changing Australia, and the world. But even those with these freedoms are hemmed in by circumstance; it's a quasi-freedom.

This is not a book about people who want desperately to have children, but can't. It doesn't deal with the heartache of medical complications or miscarriages. I won't pretend to understand the IVF rollercoaster. It's for people who have chosen childlessness, or are feeling ambivalent, or have come to terms with not having children, or are trying to. It's also for people who want to understand this demographic shift better. This is a little book about the big idea of freedom. How women, given freedom, generally end up having fewer or no children. And how that freedom is heavily qualified, hemmed in by not-freedom. The obstacles include, but are not limited to: your age, your health, your income, your wealth. Other constraints relate to whether or not you have a partner; the confines of your job and financial situation; and potential discrimination you may face when it comes to sperm donation or surrogacy if you're gay. Your support, or lack of it, also plays a part. This freedom's very restrictive limits mean women have to deal with dinner-party judging, workplace sneering and family prying into their womanly, wombly intentions.

Freedom is inexorably changing our societal makeup. Australia, this migrant nation, is increasingly reliant on those migrants as the national fertility rate dwindles. Not only are the migrants mostly young, and taxpayers, they're having kids of their own and keeping Australia's population growing as Australian-born women have fewer children. Which scares the shit out of some people, not least some people in Canberra. But no one has a clear grasp of what's really happening and what to do about it.

There are no clear data on why women choose not to have children, just listicles, angry blogs and anecdotes. Then there's the hard fact that women are having children later, through choice as they navigate education and careers, or through personal circumstance as they search for partners, negotiate with partners, or decide to go ahead without partners. That means they're having fewer children or, if it's too late, none at all.

Controversial personal choices are rubbing up against hot-button political issues—and that's bound to breed trouble.

Barren vs breeder?

Anyone who has chosen to remain deliberately barren ... they've got no idea about what life's about.

Former Liberal senator Bill Heffernan

A woman's fertility status is fruitful ground for name-calling. Particularly vindictive people choose the word 'barren' for childless women, conjuring pictures of arid fields, devoid of life, never to be tilled. Dry.

Then there's the contemptuous use of the word 'breeder' for people with children, which makes them sound like bitches on a puppy farm, held captive for their reproductive ability. Once you ditch the insults, it's still hard to settle on the right generic words to use, when a person's situation is starkly individual.

Some women are born with that intense maternal gene; since they were girls, they dreamed of having their own children. Once grown, they take any chance to sniff a newborn's head in the fruit and vegetable section, or to touch an acquaintance's swollen stomach (always be sure, people, always be sure). Others are entirely indifferent, until they're forced to feel different. They're the ones who never felt that womanly ache ('oh, my ovaries!') and have to navigate the treacherous path of being seen as not-quite-woman, with their wasted fallopian tubes. In between there's a glorious array of uncertainty, of women weighing up their entire lives and trying to work out whether, when, how many, what's possible and what's not. Most women sit somewhere along that colourful spectrum, neither eternally hungry for baby contact nor completely uninterested. Wanting, wanting to want, not wanting.

As hard as it is to understand how someone else feels all the way over on the other side, it's time we learned to empathise more, and judge less. Freedom means choices, and it seems our choices are always judged by those who've made a different one. As the choices get bigger—as we are more free—there's more judgement, and choice, and uncertainty, and regret.

Deeply personal and often complicated decisions around motherhood aren't easily discussed in a world that often seems to abhor nuance. I never really wanted children—although for a while I *wanted to want* them (because, like many women, I'm a trained people-pleaser, and babies certainly please people). I even tried for a bit, without success and without pure intention. It was the only time in my life I've been grateful for periods, so I worked out within months that I was kidding myself.

I do love the children of the people I love. If you share DNA with someone I adore, chances are I'll be quite fond of you. I'm ambivalent about the rest, and anxious when strange children are thrust at me. I never know what to do with my face when someone looks at me for approval when their toddler does something cute, but all I saw was a foreign small person plonk down on their arse.

Holding a stranger's baby makes my right eye twitch. When I was younger it was because I was worried I'd drop them, or that their little bobbleheads would bobble right off. So I never really got the hang of it. Now, my secret fear is that the child will start screaming uncontrollably as soon as it makes skin contact, and that will be seen as some sort of unspoken indication that I am, indeed, a bit witchy in my barrenness.

That puts me towards the uninterested side of the scale; I am 'voluntarily childless', according to the literature, as opposed to 'involuntarily childless'. The same literature also refers to 'circumstantially childless', and even 'socially infertile'. Then there are the 'future childed', which makes sense even though it's technically not a word. Almost be easier to start calling us Wives and Handmaids.

The increasingly accepted term for the 'voluntarily childless' is 'childfree'. It's a smug word, like being smoke-free or debt-free. Still, that's what I'll use from now on for simplicity when I'm specifically talking about the childless-by-choice. But note that the official statistics and academics tend to use 'childless' as a broad term that captures both voluntary and involuntary childlessness, so when I'm talking about research I'll use that uselessly broad term.

This is part of the problem we face: the statistics don't differentiate between the childfree and the childless. It's indicative of the shifting world we're living in that we don't even have a proper vocabulary for it yet. Our conversations are still bereft of common ground.

I lost my uterus in a tragic fishing accident

These women ultimately regret it. They're miserable ... they don't want to be childless, they want kids ... You, deep down, would rather be at home.

Men's rights extremist Gavin McInnes

I can just see the look on her face. Nostrils flared, whites of the eyes showing, lips curling in shock from my outburst. It started innocently enough.

'Have you got kids?' she asks.

'No.'

'Oh, why not?'

(I mumble something incoherent, look for more Chardonnay.)

'But aren't you married? You're with that nice what's-his-name, aren't you? Are you having problems?'

(Eyes sliding desperately around the room for some form of rescue.)

'It's not too late. You will have children, though, right?'

'Um, no.'

'Why on Earth not?'

'BECAUSE I LOST MY UTERUS IN A TRAGIC FISHING ACCIDENT.'

Hence the look of shock on her face.

I've been so close to shouting that, so many times, in the face of awkward, invasive, personal interrogations from people I barely know. (Fine, I never actually said it, but the fantasy is real). The question is usually intended as an innocent conversation starter, but the initial 'no' should serve as a warning sign. Most of all, because of how many women want children but are struggling to have them, in which case you're publicly picking at a painful scab. That question has been put to friends of mine who have been going through IVF cycles forever. Who've had repeated miscarriages. Who've frozen their eggs because they want kids but the timing hasn't worked out. Who desperately wanted kids but didn't want to do it alone, or ended up with partners who weren't so keen. Or who couldn't afford all these new 'choices'.

Every time someone asks me why I don't have kids, the idea of confessing to a stranger the actual truth of my ambivalence fills me with dread. So I cast about for a simple lie that might make them swiftly shut up. And years ago I came up with the tragic fishing accident line, which has always remained unspoken but sits in caps in my mind.

Somehow it seems less shocking than: 'Because I just never felt like it.' With the bonus of possibly making people think twice next time before poking around in the business of someone's internal organs. Like so many of the childless, I've been forced again and again to bumble through persistent questions, gripping a wineglass till it's fit to shatter.

Any 'no' without an explanation is a clear sign that the woman you are talking to doesn't want to talk about it. That woman knows how many people will judge her for that 'no', no matter what. She'll be judged for being childfree, or for not having tried harder, or for not having tried the acupuncture, or vaginal steaming. For not having tried soon enough, or for not having settled for a good-enough guy. The perfectly well-intentioned small talk quickly becomes excruciating and defensive—on both sides.

The questions about your childbearing intentions start early, gently. They build in intensity as you get older—if you get engaged or shack up with someone—and they climax if you get married. Because having a child is the 'natural' state of affairs, and throughout human history a woman's value has been proven through the productivity of her womb.

Women without children have variously been hunted as witches, seen as devil-possessed, and diagnosed with imaginary maladies of the womb that proved their inherent weakness and wiliness. The Hippocratic tradition (from the father of modern medicine) was to fix errant ('wandering') uteruses with tin or lead probes. The afflicted woman also had to eat boiled puppy, according to a report published in the *Bulletin of the History of Medicine*. The probes were used to 'try to correct the texture, aperture, and position of the womb's mouth', author Rebecca Flemming writes. 'The woman is also to drink various compounds for several days: of boiled pine twigs and white wine, and of celery, cumin seed, and frank-incense, accompanied by eating boiled

puppy and octopus, and bathing twice a day.'
Hysterical, right?

Witches were, and remain, a common
trope for the childless. Solitary older women,
feared for their unconventionality. Crones.
Occasionally, wicked stepmothers. Stealers
of other women's children. In Africa today
women can still be cast out of their commu-
nities, considered victims of witchcraft, or
be branded witches themselves if they don't
bear children. Australia's first female prime
minister, Julia Gillard, was labelled a witch,
most famously when then Opposition leader
Tony Abbott appeared at a demonstration in
front of a sign that read 'Ditch the Witch'.
Complete with broomstick.

Today in the developed world, discrimination against witchy childless women doesn't

culminate in someone getting burned at the stake, but they still face stigmas and biases. There are everyday assumptions that having children is the norm, and not having them is abnormal. Because 'normal' and 'natural' are virtuous words. Even though 'normal' is a meaningless word to apply to humanity and 'natural' excludes polyester suits and cars. Politicians, especially at budget time, bang on endlessly about families, meaning nuclear. Or 'mum and dad investors'.

When a man dies, he's usually described by his job first. If it's a woman, she's a mother first. And often, that's all. In a 2019 obituary in my paper, *The Advertiser*, under a subheading 'Family', it read 'Pam had no children'. It went on to say that Pamela Cleland was 'part of the family which built Château Tanunda', a student who was 'one of the brilliant young set of post-war Adelaide', an artist, a journalist and a ground-breaking lawyer who defended gay men when homosexuality was a crime. But she had 'no children'. No 'family'. The paper swiftly fixed it online, but it was the newspaper's default template.

This should be ancient history, this relegation of women to their wombs' function. But there's always been a stickiness to the old ways, accompanied by backlashes against feminism, and there's a new uneasiness in the world with throwback leaders preaching populist appeals for women to know their place.

The #MeToo campaign against sexual harassment and assault startled and then frightened men around the world, who felt as though all men were being tarnished by the actions of a few. This latest backlash against uppity women kicked off with #NotAllMen, which echoed through both the Twittersphere and mainstream media. Each feminist action always seems to have an opposite reaction, and the #MeToo reaction's subtext followed along the lines of 'Well, this women's freedom thing has just gone a bit too far now'. That reaction has spawned a movement pressing for a return to times when women were viewed as mothers, and mothers only.

The alt-right—a loose conglomeration of neo-Nazis, Trump-lovers, white nationalists and anti-PC warriors—is pushing for a return to 1950s womanhood. A theme of their wet dream is that women are secretly unhappy with freedom, and yearning for a return to male control. One of their revered heroes, Milo

Yiannopoulos, argues that birth control and abortion are 'the work of the Devil' and only lead to misery and suffering. He says the Pill makes women 'dangerously fat' and gives them 'cottage cheese thighs'. He says women on the Pill 'Don't look right and don't talk right', that they are sluts who choose the wrong mates.

'Thanks to your birth control, you're as attractive as a post-menopausal cat lady,' he wrote in *Breitbart*. 'Tossing out birth control isn't just kinder to women, it may be the only way to save civilisation … And hey! It's what God wants, too.' There should be no birth control, Yiannopoulos concludes after mashing together some half-baked theories, because 'we need the kids if we're to breed enough to keep the Muslim invaders at bay'. That idea has lurked in the murk in Russia and

Germany—we need women chattel breeding more of 'our' people.

Gavin McInnes, another poster boy of the alt-right movement and founder of the Proud Boys extremist chauvinist movement, calls childcare 'maternal infidelity'. Childless 'spinsters' would rather be barefoot and pregnant, he says. 'They're miserable.'

Canadian psychology professor Jordan Peterson, who insists he is not of the alt-right, but remains their darling, laments the contraceptive pill as a 'radical biological invention' that led to porn and masturbation and 'wild sexual experimentation'. Giving women control over their own fertility made them able to compete with men on a more equal footing, he argues, causing mass confusion, political upheaval and 'new females'.

These aren't Reddit fringe-dwellers typing with one hand while masturbating to the idea that one day soon women will be forced to submit to them. These are men with millions of followers between them, who tour the globe teaching young men their misogynistic ways. They reflect and are reflected by men in power. They get a spot on the ABC's *Q&A*. They are part of the backlash to women's freedom, particularly the freedom the Pill gave them.

I am loath to even mention them, really. But I have spoken at high schools, even universities, and this stuff comes up. These reprobates have struck a chord that resonates with more men than it should. We're living in a disruptive time, a whorl that threatens the status quo. These modern throwbacks are appealing to a broad base of men who feel threatened by change, and specifically by women's freedom.

Male world leaders have echoed those sentiments about the primacy of childbearing for women. US president Donald Trump, the pussy grabber, had his daughter Ivanka voice an ad telling American women that 'the most important job any woman can have is being a mother'. He says that Hallmark-card notion of Mother's Day is one of the most important days in the year.

In Russia, President Vladimir Putin is throwing money at women to encourage them to have more children, working against abortion and heaping public praise on women who care for family. He has equated having children with national security—producing more of 'our' people. Turkish President

Recep Tayyip Erdoğan has called the child-less 'half-people'.

As those male world leaders sneer at child-less women, female world leaders cop it. When Jacinda Ardern was made leader of the New Zealand Labour Party—then in opposition—she was grilled on her plans to procreate by reporters who said the public had a right to know, and questioned whether it would be okay for her to take maternity leave if she won the upcoming election. Labour went on to win the election and she was sworn in as PM in October 2017. In January 2018 she announced she was pregnant and that her husband, Clarke Gayford, would be a stay-at-home dad. She was swiftly accused by the *Daily Mail*'s Liz Jones, among others, of betraying voters. 'Surely your country shouldn't have to compete for attention with a colicky toddler,' Jones wrote. This doesn't happen the other way around.

In Australia, Liberal senator Bill Heffernan wasn't alone in labelling Labor's Julia Gillard as unfit to be prime minister because she was 'deliberately barren'. Former attorney-general George Brandis, former Labor leader Mark Latham, and former prime minister Tony Abbott all criticised Julia Gillard for being childless. Her own nemesis-slash-colleague Kevin Rudd reportedly called her a 'childless, atheist, ex-communist'. (Ms Gillard reportedly once said to then US president Barack Obama, 'You think it's tough being African-American? Try being me. Try being an atheist, childless, single woman as prime minister.')

Recent research shows that Australian women can feel socially excluded if they choose to remain childless. A study on Australian childless women published in the *Journal of Social Inclusion* in 2016 found 'pronatalism'—the pro-child nature of our society—stigmatised the childless. Pronatalism represents motherhood as a 'moral, patriotic and economic duty', as 'central to being a woman', and it marginalises 'deviant' women without children. The Deakin University study looked at a range of research and found those without children felt they were seen as 'unnatural, deficient, unfulfilled and incomplete'. 'The study further suggests circumstantially and involuntarily childless women, followed by voluntarily childless women, perceive more stigmatisation and exclusion due to being childless than undecided and future-childed women,' the article said. 'Such differences may be influenced by the nature of women's "deviance" from pronatalism.'

There are plenty of books, blogs and articles detailing the ways mothers are discriminated against; how they can be swallowed up by motherhood, excluded and forced into seclusion. A woman's identity is inextricably linked to her childbearing ability—too strongly linked. Women can't get free of it, no matter what they do, no matter how much freedom they have.

The woman herself too often is secondary to what she can produce. From the moment a woman turns down an alcoholic drink, the smirks start; and the distinction begins. Her identity starts being subsumed into her role.

There is of course a wonderful side to having children—an expansion. A new identity is born along with a new human. There is a word for this transformation: matrescence. A parallel with adolescence. The transition to motherhood, encompassing changes that affect the hormones, skin, hair. But becoming a mother is also a massive cultural shift and all the pretence that modern women can take it in their stride is an absolute farce. If anything, the pimples of adolescence were a breeze compared to perineal rupture, postnatal depression and the immense life change that takes place. And throughout this seismic disruption, women are meant to be filled with the joy of procreation, while contemplating the purchase of a Bugaboo Runner to help them become a Yummy Mummy.

Women can't win

It's depressing but possibly instructive too that women can face discrimination when applying for jobs in part because they *might* have children. Then once they're working, they can face discrimination for being childless—it's not just politicians who can be accused of lacking understanding. There are also cases of women—who might care for parents, for example—not being able to get Christmas off because they don't have children. Or they might be expected to pick up the slack because, being without offspring, they are seen as not having lives outside of work.

The same women might go on to have children, and then face discrimination as a result. A career pause in itself limits women's superannuation and chances of promotion. Returning to part-time or casual work can be a career-limiting move. The Australian Human Rights Commission has found half of working women experience discrimination while pregnant, on parental leave or on return to work. That's despite the fact there are more working mothers than ever before. The ABS says more than half of mothers now work—but despite how common the juggle is, women are still being judged no matter what they do.

Female politicians are lambasted for a perceived lack of empathy if they don't have kids, but also questioned over their parenting if they do. Childless people in workplaces might roll their eyes when parents leave at 4.59 p.m., while those parents likely feel the eye-rolls and fear the consequences of not staying late, of not being able to go to the pub with the boss or play golf with contacts, of getting a dreaded call from childcare in the early afternoon.

A group of women without children might meet at a trendy bar, toasting their freedom while secretly resenting that they never see their mother-friends. Meanwhile the mother-friends might be posting Facebook pictures of their children's Halloween costumes, while shedding a quiet tear that they no longer get invited to drinks with their old friends.

The childless may sometimes yearn for the childfull life, while the childfull may occasionally envy the freedom of the child-less. It's enough to make you wish for a magic wand and a witchy broomstick.

Oh, come on, you'll change your mind—the clock is ticking!

Having children is the great loving experience of a lifetime. And, by definition, you haven't got as much love in your life if you make that particular choice.

Former Labor leader Mark Latham

At work a while back I was complaining that the air con—usually set to sub zero—was turned up to practically balmy. No one else agreed; my mate reached for the emergency nanna rug we keep in the office.

'Huh,' I said. 'Must be the menopause.'

There was a heartbeat of silence and mortified looks from younger colleagues before I guffawed, thereby showing them that it was just a hilarious joke and I was nowhere near that age. Then I googled the average age of menopause just to be sure. (It's fifty-one.) I'm in my early forties, so safe from the 'change of life' for a bit, but if I suddenly decided to have kids, me and my ancient eggs would probably be in for a torrid time. Not many women my age conceive easily; most need assisted reproductive technologies such as IVF or donated eggs. The chances of someone my age getting pregnant naturally are miniscule, and all the technology in the world only raises the likelihood to tiny.

So it's endlessly surprising when people tell me I'll change my mind. Uber drivers, a

GP, once even a woman-child working in a clothing store who looked about twelve. I'd like to think it's my youthful good looks. But it's not. It's disbelief that I'm not still striving to quicken.

Some people find it so hard to believe I don't want a child that they insist on referring to my dog as a furbaby (not the people I know; they're just slightly impressed I can keep something alive besides succulents). But those people who don't know me so well like to think that the furball is a replacement baby. He's not. I love that dog, but he's a dog. Sure, I tickle his tummy and of course I get him vaccinated—but he's still a dog. I mean, I had him castrated, leave him alone all day, and feed him liver treats. He's a dog, not a replacement baby.

The subtext of 'you'll change your mind' goes back to the idea of motherhood being the natural position and anything else being deviant. That in turn means that the childless must be locked in battle against the mythical biological clock. That hormones will eventually ensure the right instinct kicks in. That a proper woman will at some point gasp and realise she is destined for children. (Hey, if she does, *do not* get smug on her pregnant arse. That's just rude.)

The idea that some hormonal clock makes us go gaga for babies at a specific time is cuckoo. A woman might have an epiphany about childlust, but that epiphany did not spring fully formed from her loins. We have circadian rhythms, which are unrelated to reproduction. We have monthly cycles, which are related to fertility but not to childlust. We have a drive for sex. And there's a 'clock' counting down to our infertility. But there's no spontaneous, natural internal change that makes women *suddenly* want a baby.

Research has shown that 'baby fever' exists in both men and women but is not related to any sort of out-of-the-blue hormonal surge. Kansas State University published findings of a study into this topic in the journal *Emotion* in 2011. They found exposure to good baby experiences such as cuddles increased the desire to have babies, while negative expo-sure such as listening to a baby's piercing cries decreased it. Then rational factors such as considering the trade-offs of having babies kicked in. 'We had people who were high on the positive aspects and they see all the good things about babies and want a baby,' psychology professor and co-author Gary Brase said. 'We also had people who were high on the negative aspects and absolutely do not want to have babies. Then we had people who were high on both positive and negative aspects and were very conflicted about children.

'Having children is kind of the reason we exist—to reproduce and pass our genes on to the next generation,' he said. 'But economically, having children is expensive and you don't get any decent financial return on this investment. And yet, here we are, actual people kind of stuck in the middle.'

'The reason we exist' is a biological argument; it's true, but it's not the whole story. People want to pass on their genes; the end of your family's bloodline seems unbearably sad—but that's not particularly rational. Unless your bloodline includes the DNA for altruism, your blood holds the cure to cancer, or your genes mean you can wear your underpants on the outside and save innocent lives, it is just a thread in an unimaginably large tapestry.

There's also an instinct to pass on what you know. I do it sometimes—imagine how I would love to share the occasional insight I have about life. How I learned that it's a bad idea to grab Dad's old razor and rub it up and down your legs vigorously because your friends are shaving theirs. I would like to tell my nieces one day that ribbons of skin and unstoppable bleeding in the name of vanity is a very poor idea. Every time I read a good book, or discover a hidden travel gem, or work out how to drill a hole in brick, I feel the urge to share that. To help someone who doesn't know. (Just as well we have Twitter, then.)

Amid the plethora of superficial reasons for having children, women are in the main making their choices based on deep thinking, driven by their circumstances. Hopefully their choices are increasingly honed by supportive information, rather than arsehole assumptions.

Of course plenty of women change their minds. And many never do. But if you untangle this oft-heard expression, 'You'll change your mind', there's a sort of desperate hope to it. The people saying 'You'll change your mind' want reassurance that ultimately, given time, everyone will come to the same conclusion they have. Otherwise you're implicitly challenging their decision, and their subconscious baulks at that.

It is true and right that women (and men) change their minds. Babylust can wax and wane. They might change their minds multiple times as different costs and benefits become apparent. They might find themselves surrounded by friends with babies and realise they want that sort of fulfilment. They might find a new relationship that suddenly makes the idea irresistible. Heterosexual or homosexual couples or single women might find a way to have babies that they hadn't found before. The woman who desperately wanted kids early may get over it; another could have the instinct grow to the point where she will think about unprotected sex with strangers just to get there. It's not a magical internal tide; it comes and goes with stages of life, with other satisfactions, losses, jealousies or comparisons.

But strangers telling women that they'll change their minds shows how much having children is still considered essential to being a woman; that if you don't, you'll fall short. It's saying, in the words of Erdoğan, that you are 'lacking', 'deficient' and 'half a person'. Which is why that phrase can induce a hot flush of rage. It's saying that while you're free, you're morally wrong.

Who isn't doing their bit?

*If we want women of that calibre to have
families, and we should, well, we have to give
them a fair dinkum chance to do so.*
Former prime minister Tony Abbott on
high-income, educated women

Australia is having a baby bust. The statistics show the fertility rate of 1.74 is falling. The data show that women are leaving it later in life to have kids, which tends to mean they have fewer babies overall, and that an increasing number of families are never having children at all. According to the latest statistics, the median age of mothers in 2017 was 31.3, up from 30.7 a decade before that. In 1977 it was 26.1.

'The long-term decline in fertility of younger mums as well as the continued increase in fertility of older mums reflects a shift towards late childbearing,' ABS demography director Anthony Grubb says. 'Together, this has resulted in a rise in [the] median age of mothers and a fall in Australia's total fertility rate.'

Just to keep the population levels up in the absence of immigration the fertility rate needs to be 2.1—that's called the replacement rate. So two babies on average per woman (plus a little buffer) to replace those who are dying. Not that long ago (well, about a century) the fertility rate was four.

Certain groups of immigrants are still having plenty of babies—the highest fertility rates are in women born in Lebanon, Africa, Pakistan, Laos and Syria. But these are tiny populations in Australia, so their higher fertility rates are irrelevant in terms of the effect on the average rate. It's only interesting because the biggest global study of fertility rates—the *Lancet* study mentioned earlier—gives us a very solid understanding of how culture affects the number of children women have. The *Lancet* study found most countries with high fertility rates—more than three children per woman in 2017—are in sub-Saharan Africa, North Africa and the Middle East. The study found that fertility rates ranged from 7.1 in Niger, West Africa, to one in Cyprus. The authors found the countries with high fertility rates were those where women could not get adequate contraception. You can imagine why. Less freedom, more babies. They found three key factors that influenced fertility rates:

- **Education.** Please note: the strong connection between more education and fewer children doesn't mean stupid people are breeding; this is not *Idiocracy*. It's two-fold. As countries allow more equality in education for women, that equates to more empowerment for women. And in countries where more women are attaining higher levels of education, they're making different choices about motherhood.
- **Contraception.** Availability of adequate contraceptive choices is self-explanatory.

To be clear: if women have no contraception, they don't have freedom. So they have more babies.

- **Child mortality.** In those parts of the world where women have it the hardest, they tend to have more babies who die. So they have more. Fewer babies dying means fewer babies overall. This is one of the most depressing statistics I've ever heard.

The point, again, is freedom. Better conditions for women mean fewer babies. Report author Professor Christopher Murray, from the University of Washington, said half the world's countries now have fertility rates below replacement level. He called it a 'surprise', and a 'remarkable transition'. Professor Murray urged people to think about the consequences of a society with more grandparents than grandchildren. 'On current trends there will be very few children and lots of people over the age of 65 and that's very difficult to sustain.'

Back in Australia, the ABS data show that the number of people living in couple families with children has gone from being the majority to a steadily declining minority. Statistics from 2011 showed that the number of couple families without children would overtake the number of couple families with children to become the most common family type in Australia sometime between 2023 and 2029, and pointed to decisions about delaying childbearing or not having children at all as the cause.

The 2016 data winds that prediction back a bit but shows a clear trend of fewer couple

families living with children. 'The increase
in people living in couple families without children was not consistent across age
groups. Between 1996 and 2016 the propor-
tion increased among 25 to 34 year olds and
decreased among 45 to 59 year olds, reflect-
ing the trend of women delaying childbirth,'
ABS director of demography, Anthony
Grubb, said.

This global demographic shift means
in general, developed countries—where
women have more freedom—are seeing
fewer births. That brings the threat of
declining populations. Meanwhile devel-
oping countries—where women have less
freedom—have birth rates far above
replacement levels, bringing the threat of
uncontrolled population growth.

So there are baby booms in countries that can't afford them, and baby busts in countries that need more young people. Just as well there's migration to start settling those differences, but that has become a scorching political topic with the rise of nationalistic governments around the world. Europe has been startled by waves of refugees, the United States has elected a nationalistic, xenophobic leader, and Australia has always suffered politically febrile conversations about immigration.

Australia's situation is further complicated by the concentration of immigrants in the big cities—so in Sydney they're bitching about traffic congestion while in country South Australia they're crying out for more people. And there's a stark difference in Aboriginal and Torres Strait Islander populations—their fertility rate is 2.33, and the median age of registering a birth is 25.6 years, about six years lower than the national median. The socioeconomic differences are stark, but ignored, and no one is talking about why.

Social conditions affecting women's freedom over their own bodies and therefore their own choices have snowballed to become global concerns. But it's not up to women to fix this with their personal choices.

Why aren't they doing their bit?

People who want children are all alike.
People who don't want children don't want them in their own ways.

US author Meghan Daum reimagines
Leo Tolstoy's well-known words

Just imagine a 2026 census question:

How many children have you had?

If you have none, please select a reason …

This is data we need, but don't have. We know quite a bit about why men and women physiologically cannot have children, but diddly squat about why they don't in the absence of medical factors. We know that a cohort of women are leaving it too late, and we know that more women are choosing not to have kids—but we really don't yet have the stats on their reasons.

Dr Bronwyn Harman is a senior lecturer at Edith Cowan University. She's in the thick of a PhD on attitudes to childlessness in Australia. 'We know approximately 25 per cent of all women aged between fifteen and twenty-four [now] will never have children,' she says. 'We think about two thirds of those are voluntarily childfree—but it's hard to tell.'

Imagine the boxes following that census question:

I hate children.

I can't afford children.

I can't afford the reproductive technology.

I just never felt the urge.

I sort of liked kids but then my friend had a child with special needs and it scared the crap out of me.

I don't have a partner and single parents do it tough.

I'm gay and the system sucks.

I didn't think about it because I was too focused on work and now it's too late unless I fork out thousands for IVF and I just don't care that much.

I can't afford IVF.

I don't want to give up my annual holiday to Ibiza.

I broke up with my partner at thirty-eight and am not sure how to put 'must have babies soon' on my Tinder profile.

My partner wasn't into it and I didn't want to nag.

My own childhood traumatised me.

I lost my uterus in a tragic fishing accident.

It's a statistical nightmare.

Dr Harman uses the words 'childless' and 'childfree' to differentiate between those who would like a baby but don't have one, and those who don't want them, but concedes they are inadequate terms to describe the gamut of personal experiences. Her research is looking at the childfree, specifically. She is passionate about hosing down bullshit theories about the childfree. 'Very few actively dislike children. There's a myth that people who don't have children voluntarily don't like children. That's not true at all,' she said. 'Somebody told me it's like having a Lamborghini. They don't actually want one, they just want to drive one every now and then.' That seems materialistic, but it matches the stories of many non-childbearers who love children. They just want to hand them back, and not have the bother permanently.

Dr Harman said another myth is that women who don't want children must have suffered themselves in childhood. The evidence shows that's not true, she said. There's not a traumatised anti-kid thing. Just a *meh*-kid thing. After that ambivalence—let's call it kidnosticism—she says another reason for not reproducing is the accompanying loss of freedom. 'Whether that's financial, physical, emotional, or psychological freedom.'

It's categorically true that kids are expensive little time-stealers. Not their fault, it just means there is a cost-benefit analysis done alongside any emotional instincts that potential parents have, and that sometimes end in a 'no, thanks'. But the idea that the childless are spending their weekends chortling at the stupid breeders while skiing in Thredbo is an unhelpful stereotype. (Even if it may happen from time to time.) Most weekends, the childless are more likely to be working, or hanging out with nieces and nephews, or looking after stepchildren, or their ageing parents.

Childfree couples mostly don't hate kids. According to Zoë Krupka, from La Trobe University, some women 'simply want a different kind of life'. And in many cases it's 'the degraded state and overinflated expectations of motherhood' most are not keen on. That is a fascinating indictment of stereotypes perpetuated in our society. Advertisements, media and particularly social media promote the notion that motherhood is easy, blessed, calm and sacred. In reality, most mothers would cough up their long-awaited, end-of-the-day gin and tonic at that idea.

Unrealistic expectations could be playing a part in women opting out of the whole game. In *Selfish, Shallow and Self-Absorbed: Sixteen writers on the decision not to have kids*, edited by Meghan Daum, Laura Kipnis throws the gauntlet down on the history of maternal instincts. She argues that those instincts are not in fact 'natural' but culturally conceived. She traverses history, outlining the 'romance' of having children as stemming from the switch from when high infant mortality made children more disposable, to when they became more 'precious'. 'It was only when children's actual economic value declined, because they were no longer necessary additions to the household labor force, that they became the priceless little treasures we know them as today,' she writes. '[It] took a decline in infant mortality rates for mothers to start regarding their offspring with much affection.'

Her eyebrow-raising argument is that once it cost more to have kids, as opposed to sending kids out to make money for the household, their emotional value increased as their economic value decreased. Biological instinct, she says, is a 'culturally specific development, not a fact of nature'. In other words, children used to be an economic option—when you needed a brood of chimneysweepers—but became a romantic privilege. Their individual value has increased. She delights in giving a little *fuck you* 'to a society that sentimentalises children except when it comes to allocating enough resources to raising them'. Harsh, but fair.

In the same book, Kate Christensen, after a convoluted, painful, tortuous time, describes lying awake, asking herself 'Where are my children?' She talks about an 'old mourning for the babies I'd never had'. But she too waxed and waned, wanted then didn't, was married, then wasn't. And, eventually, she had 'not even a twinge' for children.

What about men?

You don't think of men getting broody, but that's exactly what was happening to me. I was watching my friends start their own families and thinking: why should they have everything I've always wanted?
Robin Hadley, a UK academic who went on to write a PhD on childless men

Although the word 'broody' makes one think of mopey chickens, Dr Hadley makes a good point. His thesis is that men and women have equal levels of desire for parenthood, but that men have a more isolating experience of childlessness because there's no narrative for them.

That lack of narrative is due, at least in part, to the lack of male-specific statistics. The female stats are sparse; it's even worse with males. Men are harder to track because they don't actually do the physical heavy lifting of childbirth, so official statistics give the fertility rate based on the number of children per woman.

They're also left out of the public narrative because while women's identities are entwined with their motherhood status, men's identities are untethered from children to a large extent. Women have been made slaves to their bodies, to its ebbs and flows. Even in their modern-day freedom, they are enslaved, while men are freer. From puberty, women are captured by their fertility cycles, while men mark theirs by wet dreams, pimples, and hair in new places. We are more marked by our transitions than men.

Men, on the other hand, appear to sail through almost obliviously when it comes to their age. At the same time that magazines are writing about 'Sad Jen' missing the baby boat, they're celebrating Mick Jagger having his eighth kid at seventy-three. Sad Jen is done for, she's missed the boat. Because women have a use-by date, while men can keep spreading successful seed forever. The research shows that's not true; both sperm and eggs go off with age, but that's not the narrative you read about in the media, where grey hair makes a man distinguished and a woman 'past it'.

Men may be seen as unlucky in love, or as unfortunate in sperm, or as a glamorous and slick bachelor. But they're rarely seen as 'unnatural' in the way women are. Childless women are barren spinsters. Childless men are roguish, independent—and still eligible. Or so go the stereotypes. There is an assumption that men are voluntarily childless, when many of them have also been hit with the infertility stick. As with women, though, all childless people are lumped in together statistically so it's hard to find a clear picture.

What is clear is that women have more freedom when it comes to having a child on their own. It's much easier to find willing sperm than willing uteruses. A woman can—not without risk—get impregnated with no relationship in sight: unprotected sex, online sperm, artificial insemination. They just need the gamete to get on with it, while men face far greater challenges.

Medical technology is geared towards the female as part of this grand assumption that a female has a right (and maybe even a duty) to reproduce. The same rigid thinking that decries a childfree woman gives the yearning woman more options, while men have few.

And while women have a keen appreciation of the fertility cliff, men still hang on to the Jagger-like dream of never-ending virility. Unlike men, women are consistently reminded of their timelines. Women have a countdown to the Fertility Apocalypse thrust upon them. We know to look out for a hot flush, a sign things are nearly done.

IVF is sometimes a saviour for late childlust, but it's not a balm for the age-infertile; past a certain point, it can't help. The University of Adelaide's Professor Rob Norman, one of Australia's top fertility experts, says women have mostly realised that IVF is no safety net, but men still drag their heels. 'I often see patients where a woman's been willing to have a child but the husband says it's not time yet,' he said.

One side effect of women being accosted from a young age about childbearing is that they're more likely to be hyperaware of how it all works; men can stay blissfully ignorant for longer. For too long. That means they're not driving a conversation about it, so the conversation often simply isn't happening.

No wonder men are brooding about it.

Isn't it better to have fewer people?

I encourage people who can, if you have the opportunity, if you're young enough, to have one for mum, one for dad and one for the country.

Then treasurer Peter Costello in 2002 after introducing the baby bonus

What an abysmal abdication of responsibility to make it sound like a woman's duty to fix the country's population situation. Successive governments have failed to come up with a coherent population policy, or to deal with the twin issues of the falling fertility rate and the booming immigration rate. They want population growth to keep the economy ticking along, but there's nothing like a Sydney or Melbourne traffic jam to piss off voters. People in those congested cities are not the only ones irate at the idea of continual growth.

The Voluntary Human Extinction Movement's members would have been chuffed to see the *Lancet* results on plummeting fertility. The environmental group's motto is 'May we live long and die out'. You can get it on a bumper sticker. 'Phasing out the human race by voluntarily ceasing to breed will allow Earth's biosphere to return to good health. Crowded conditions and resource shortages will improve as we become less dense … each time another one of us decides to not add another one of us to the burgeoning billions already squatting on this ravaged planet, another ray of hope shines through the gloom,' it says on its website.

For a more sensible take, listen to Sustainable Population Australia. SPA concedes it's not individual actions that will solve the population puzzle—they want governments to do something about immigration. They're worried about the strain a big population puts on Australia, and its resources, environment and infrastructure, and the contribution this makes to climate change. There are valid arguments for taking the small population approach—particularly in the current vacuous absence of a climate change policy. Recent governments have been trying to birth a policy that breeches the gap between market demand and immigration-phobia, while facing the painful contractions of declining fertility and the expanding demand for affordable and accessible childcare.

There are ethical implications to filling up our country and sucking it dry, and politicians generally have a bad track record at a) managing population increases sustainably and b) dealing with issues around immigration with cool heads. There's also the incontrovertible fact that population growth drives the economy. What political party, enslaved to short-term cycles, would want to interrupt economic growth? Pity the poor pollie who knows that immigration boosts the GDP, but also knows that everyday punters blame immigration for everything from those traffic jams to unemployment. Add to that the public perception—aided and abetted by some politicians—that it's somehow refugees boosting the numbers, when they're only a fraction of our immigrant intake. (Remember Fiona Scott, who won the Liberal seat of Lindsay at the 2013 election, vacantly asserting '[Asylum seekers are] a hot topic here because our traffic is overcrowded'?)

For years Australia has lacked a coherent population policy, while all these factors are playing out. Our leaders seem incapable of having rational conversations about immigration without dog whistling or outright race baiting, and the population debate gets endlessly mired in furphies. Further complexity is added by the uneven distribution of migrants and the push to make them

settle in smaller cities or regional areas—
a concession to the belief that we still need
more people, just in specific places. The
federal government (the Coalition, at the
time of writing) wants to decide not only
who comes to this country and the circumstances in which they come, but also where
they settle.

Australia is in the midst of a demographic
shift: our fertility rate is dropping but we are
more than making up for that with immigration, and because we are living longer. Thanks
to the ABS, here's a snapshot of our population clock the day we hit 25 million people on
8 August 2018. In Australia, there is:

- one birth every one minute and forty-two
  seconds

- one death every three minutes and sixteen seconds
- one person arriving to live here every 1 minute and 1 second
- one Australian resident leaving to live overseas every 1 minute and 51 seconds.

Add to that complex mix the fact that we are an ageing population, with the potential for a dwindling pool of taxpayers to support an ageing pool of pensioners—although we can hope that they'll be healthier for longer, and therefore contribute tax for longer.

The ABS also points out we have almost 4000 people over the age of 100. ('That's a lot of letters from the Queen,' the normally bone-dry statistics bods note.) A more relevant statistic, from the 2016 census, is that the number of people aged over sixty-five has increased from one in twenty-five a century ago, to one in six now. Meanwhile immigrants tend to be younger, which helps offset the ageing demographic.

One of the nation's top demographers, Emeritus Professor Peter McDonald from the Australian National University, says, 'The point about migration is that it's not just about the migrants, it's the migrants' children. Migrants that come to Australia are quite young on average. They haven't had their children.

'What migration does is change the age structure of the population and that means there are more people in the working ages than there would be otherwise and that brings all sorts of benefits to the economy— including fiscal benefits.'

There are high moral arguments from people who weave their own hemp jumpsuits from leftover cannabis fibres about having fewer people on this land, but the truth is that for the vast majority, the decision to have children is driven by love, gut instinct, luck and timing. And the decision *not* to is unlikely to be solely based on environmental grounds. (A highly flawed survey released in 2019 claimed a third of women under thirty were thinking about not having children because of climate change; but the survey was only of women who were supporters of environmental groups. That number dropped significantly as women hit thirty.)

It's the government's responsibility to get the population policy settings right, sort out the immigration plan, and support individuals in whatever procreation choices they make. And to work out an effective climate change policy that doesn't leave anyone feeling they're the problem.

But if I don't wipe someone's bum, who will wipe mine?

Motherhood has most definitely changed me and my life ... even silly things, like the fact that all of my pictures on my cell phone used to be of me at photo shoots ... but now every single picture on my phone is of Mason.

Famous-for-something woman
Kourtney Kardashian

Won't someone please think of the childless?

Liberal Democratic Party's
David Leyonhjelm

In Japan, adult nappies now outsell baby nappies. Japan is resistant to immigration, has one of the lowest fertility rates in the world, and the Japanese live for a bloody long time. A perfect storm.

So the population is declining. This is leaving them with a shrinking workforce and, therefore, tax base. More people needing healthcare, fewer people to pay for it. Japan is fertile ground for population discussions. There are even companies there dedicated to cleaning up after people who die alone, and rot. They have a name for it. *Kodokushi*. Which may sound like an ascetic cleaning philosophy but is the Japanese word for a lonely death. It is a far cry from KonMari, Marie Kondo's cult cleaning program that tells people to ask whether their objects 'spark joy'. There are no joy sparks here.

Loneliness is the stuff of mournful songs and deep-seated terror. Being alone, dying alone. I live alone and in dark moments have wondered how long it would take someone to notice if I was no longer around—if I tumbled headlong down the stairs, would people mistake my absence for my occasional introversion? What if I became the star of one of those stories where people only get found once they start to smell? Or because my hungry hound wouldn't stop howling, prompting the neighbours to investigate?

Crikey, better get cracking on the childbearing.

Japanese prime minister Shinzō Abe has been talking about increasing the retirement age. The notoriously insular nation is even looking at bringing workers in—albeit temporarily. European countries too are increasing or planning to increase their retirement ages.

Japan's politicians keep calling for women to have more babies. The first clarion call came from the then health minister Hakuo Yanagisawa back in 2007 when he described women as 'birth-giving machines' who should be doing their best to stop the falling birthrate.

The word 'selfish' gets bandied around when it comes to childlessness. As though a woman should be bearing children to fulfil a national duty. In *Shallow, Selfish and Self-Absorbed*, Lionel Shriver—the author of *We Need To Talk About Kevin*, a harrowing tale about raising a serial-killer child that might well put the ambivalent off having kids—could not give less of a shit about appearing 'selfish'. 'They are untidy; they would have messed up my apartment. In the main, they are ungrateful. They would have siphoned too much time away from the writing of my precious books,' she says. It's a very specific antagonism, and not one that's echoed in the research. Mostly women who choose not to have kids don't cite their apartment's cleanliness. The decision is set in the broader context of their lives, and a conscious ordering of priorities. We are all just bumbling through trying to make the best of what we have, and worrying about what it means in the short, medium and long term. Everyone is selfish in the sense that individuals weigh up the costs and benefits of any major life decision. Decisions are almost always selfish.

Women—in Australia, at least—may be freer than they ever have been to make a choice about children. But it's never been more fraught, with so many people believing they have the right to weigh in on the levels of self-interest involved in making such a private decision. Despite Costello—and many other leaders—preaching about doing one's duty for the country, outside of religious cults that wear homespun cotton and subjugate women to child-bearing, child-raising and house-cleaning, there would be few people who would honestly describe having children as a pious, selfless endeavour. The idea is ludicrous when you see the modern level of romanticisation of children, the worship of the mother and the frenzy to fit tykes out in the latest OshKosh B'gosh hooded shirt and jogger set. Some have even argued that the selfish barren are propping up the breeders with their childless taxpaying ways.

Liberal Democrats senator David Leyonhjelm gave a typically shit-stirring speech in the Senate in 2015 on the introduction of the 'no jab, no pay' policy on vaccination. 'To the childless people of Australia, I want to say, on behalf of this parliament, thank you for being childless,' he said. 'You work for more years and become more productive than the rest of Australia. You pay thousands and thousands of dollars more tax than other Australians. You get next to no welfare … but you pay when other people get pregnant, you pay when they give birth, you pay when they stay at home to look after their offspring.' The man has shown himself to be a repulsive misogynist, so we'll just let that stand as an example of how bitter things can get when the word 'selfish' gets bandied around. If private health insurance doesn't cover everything and my superannuation doesn't keep me off the pension, I'll need people's taxpaying children to keep me off dog food. So thank you, those of you who bear those children.

Obviously, women's increased freedom in relation to childbearing has become a divisive, spittingly angry issue. In *Shallow, Selfish and Self-Absorbed*, Shriver goes on to blame an increasingly individualistic culture. She argues that children are the 'biggest social casualty' of that shift. 'Children, who have converted from requirement to option, like heated seats for your car,' she writes.

'However rewarding at times, raising children can also be hard, trying, and dull, inevitably ensnaring us in those sucker values of self-sacrifice and duty.'

There is no way to objectively break down who is the most selfish in the childhood industry. Is it the childfree, who blithely resist the pressure, and spend their life putting themselves first? (While in reality often putting others first, such as ageing parents, community groups or employers. But who also risk having no one to care for them when they're old.) Is it the childless, who might use taxpayer funds to go through fruitless IVF or artificial insemination treatments? (While society encourages them to do all they can.) Is it the parents, to whom much welfare and public approval flows? (While they are creating the next generation and often navigating the work–life conundrum.)

The answer is clearly none of the above. Everyone is making selfish choices; there are far better scales to judge people on than whether or not they have pushed a melon-sized human out of their vagina. Anyway, it might not matter what you choose when it comes to reproduction—things could go to shit anyway. Relationships break up, and children can be arseholes, dysfunctional and even abusive. Personal finance, random circumstance and unavoidable vulnerabilities can leave us isolated.

Some say it's selfish to be childfree, others think it's self-indulgent to worship motherhood. The childfree are accused of selfishness, while simultaneously being asked who will look after them when they're old and infirm. As though there's a karmic paradox—you were too selfish to wipe someone's bum, so you will have no one to wipe yours. Critics are just people who've made different choices and are judging those who are different. It's also unbearably (if unconsciously) cruel to remind someone they might be alone in their old age because of the choices they've made about kids—or partnering up in general. To suggest to a person (who may already be fretting about geriatric falls) that they'll die alone and unloved just because they've made a different choice—well, that takes a special kind of selfishness.

What should we do?

It's a tough problem to root out.
Unintentionally hilarious quote from
US pastor Taffi Dollar on gender inequality and
the national birth rate

Get your rosaries off my ovaries.
Feminist chant against religious
(Catholic) interference

Talking about the taxpayer base is a pretty
clinical approach to a very personal issue—
but increasingly there are cool-headed
approaches to the issue in academic circles,

if not political ones. Medical, political, demographic approaches. All of which meld together to reinforce the idea that something needs to be done to fix the errant wander towards childlessness. Stop the womb drought.

It emerged recently that the only reason women have a seven-day break from the Pill is because back in the day the Pill's creators wanted to placate the pope. There's no scientific, medical reason for that break. It was introduced as a kowtowing compromise—the inventors of the Pill wanted to convince the Vatican that women were still having their womanly cycles, to get the pontiff's approval. It didn't work, but this damaging and weird pattern persisted. As a result, women often kept having painful periods, all the inconvenience of monthly bleeding, and an increased chance of unwanted pregnancy because men in power wanted the approval of other men in power. Another case of men still refusing to get their rosaries off our ovaries. Scientists now dismiss the break as the 'Pope Rule', and the health guidelines in the United Kingdom were officially updated in early 2019 to dispel the myth that the break was necessary.

The Catholic Church has lost its authority, not least because of the recent revelations of child sex abuse surrounding it. But governments still do the political equivalent of waving their rosaries around our ovaries. They're just trying to be subtle about it. When they talk about the dwindling fertility rate— which is rare—and are forced to concede just how much we need our immigrants, they talk childcare and workplace flexibility but mostly as sales pitches. They're loath to discuss the fertility rate because there's no three-word slogan to go with that. So they go with pronatalist policies as though they're an act of pure benevolence (with the bonus of being vote winners) while the issue of our lack of babies is ... absent. Winning votes is about baby-kissing, and it's unclear what, if anything, they'll ever do to win over the babyless.

Dr Bronwyn Harman, the senior lecturer at Edith Cowan University whose PhD is looking at attitudes towards 'childfreedom' in Australia, says pronatalist policies—prioritising the womb work—are not the answer. 'Not everybody wants to have children. Pronatalism is actually the issue in itself,' she says. 'Pronatalism in Australia is the expected ideal that women will grow up, have children. That's apparently what we do, and policies and media and public opinion reinforce that view.

'A lot of people aren't going to have children no matter what the government does. We're going to have an old population that cannot be financially supported.'

There's a range of demographers who say the government should be hands off. A series of papers in *Australian Population Studies* argue that it's not up to the government to change things, only to deal with market forces where there are limited skilled shortages. Dr Harman says the government should be reminded that it's working beyond its remit. 'It should pull its head in,' she says.

'First of all, it could be reminded that having children is not the be all for all women or all men. They don't have to have children. Often people who don't have children have other contributions to society, like volunteering or looking after relatives.'

Even though Australia's attempts to encourage women to have more children come across as paternalistic fumbling, and even though politicians pander endlessly to populism when trying to formulate population policies, we'll probably be fine, thanks to immigrants.

But, imagine for a moment if a hypothetical anti-immigration party wins government. Or wins enough power in Canberra to dictate our population policy. Let's call them the Ban Immigration Groups Official Team. If the BIGOTs win, and slash immigration, we'll be in quite a quandary. About six in ten people added to Australia's population numbers are migrants. A clear majority. The minority contribution to our population comprises babies born here. Fiddle with those stats and our population numbers start to dwindle. The top of the demographic pyramid—the old—starts to swell like an arthritic knuckle. The bottom shrinks, like a wasted muscle. It becomes disproportionate. More adult nappies, fewer babies. Maybe the BIGOTs will start a Breed For Australia program. A three-child policy. A souped-up campaign telling women that they were born to breed. Free tea towels for women who do their national duty.

The United States has seen its population propped up with migration—but the migrant numbers are falling. And a big wall—both the physical and the political kind—could act as a pretty impenetrable prophylactic. Simultaneously, the country is having a red hot go at repealing women's abortion rights. *Roe v. Wade* is back on the agenda and conservatives are still using sneaky tactics to define foetuses as babies—although this is clearly more about a) controlling women's bodies or b) religious fanaticism than it is about boosting the fertility rate. Particularly because the administration has already revoked overseas aid for family planning, and President Donald Trump comes across as someone who doesn't give the slightest shit about the fertility rate in Africa.

US congressman Steve King weighed in on his country's demographic shift with the observation that 'we can't restore our civilisation with somebody else's babies'. Increasing the numbers of the master race sounds like it could be a BIGOT policy. There's a far-right group in Germany who, in the lead-up to the 2017 election, urged women to outbreed Muslims. 'New Germans? We'll make them ourselves', was the slogan.

Suddenly a dystopian narrative where those women who are still fertile are carrying children for the increasingly infertile doesn't seem like your weekend streaming binge. Maybe the rulers of the future will take a more-carrot-than-stick approach. Maybe they'll come up with rolled-gold parental leave schemes, free childcare for all, flexible employment rules, more tax incentives. But that doesn't fix the problem either.

Scandinavian countries with strikingly family-friendly policies—which notably often

include supporting fathers to take leave—
still have below-replacement population
levels. South Korea—another country where
the government is freaking out about the lack
of babies—has been throwing money at the
problem. Baby bonuses, free childcare, leave
for both parents. It's not working. Women
these days, huh? You give them all the maternal leave in the world, and they *still* choose to
have just a couple. Or one. Or none. That's
where freedom gets you.

Short of China's one-child policy, there is
very little governments can do that changes
that fertility rate by much. In 2002 Liberal
treasurer Peter Costello exhorted women to
'have one for mum, one for dad and one for
the country'. But it's not clear if his pompous
plea, or his Baby Bonus, did the trick; there

was a mini-boom for a bit, but then it trickled off again.

Professor Norman says we'll still end up with more grandparents than grandchildren. 'We're getting into dangerous territory,' he says. 'I think it's a drift that's going to keep going.'

Other countries have the very opposite problem with their unfettered population growth. The difference has become more pronounced; as some countries wane, others wax. But there's nothing we can really learn from them, in a policy sense. You'd have to take away women's freedom—their education and access to contraception. Women's march towards equality has inexorably changed society in ways that might be unexpected, and are certainly thorny.

Reactionaries—like Jordan Peterson and his ilk—cast back in panic to simpler times when men were men and women were child-bearing machines. But there's no going back, no matter the conservative daydream.

In the end

A woman who refuses maternity and gives up housekeeping faces the threats of losing her freedom. She is lacking and is a half [a person] no matter how successful she is in the business world.

Turkish president Recep Tayyip Erdoğan

I've been swimming around in all these threads of the motherhood story for years, and have a yearning for answers. I'm used to having conclusions—I mostly write features or opinion columns based on scientific evidence, and the conclusions are usually along the lines of: vaccinate. Fluoridate. Tackle climate change.

So I have no idea how to finish this, except to say: please untether women from motherhood. Recognise that all women are entire unto themselves, whatever they do. Motherhood is one amazing thing they do; it's not all they do.

When a woman dies, don't call her a mother first, before everything else that makes up her life. Unless she at some point has said that motherhood is what defines her.

Recognise the complexities of a woman's choices, and whether she has a choice at all. Recognise how freedom can be a gilded cage. And it's about time we got some better data about why women choose childlessness, or exactly how it is thrust upon them. We need to understand this, and to find a nuanced way to look at childfree women and couples, and the childless by circumstance.

Stop saying 'As a mother' as though mothers have a moral superiority. Stop asking women why they're not having kids, or why they're not having more, or why they chose not to buy pink headbands.

Genuinely seek out your unconscious bias about motherhood. Have you ever hesitated to hire a woman of child-bearing age? Do you think she's going to be a part-time worker, even when she's full time? Have you ever given the stink-eye to a mother who leaves the office on time? Did you ever call Sophie in accounts a 'spinster'?

Government intervention struggles to be anything but paternalistic, misguided or so superficial it doesn't touch the sides of the inhibitors on actual reproductive freedom. Demographics have changed, are changing and are continuing to change and we need to talk about that with clear minds.

And, more individually, it's unclear if, in this very recent freedom women have, there are many women at all without at least a little cache of regret. What if? What if I hadn't? What if I had? What if I'd had more, sooner? What if I hadn't waited? What if I hadn't waited for perfect, or even pretty close? These are all big sliding-door moments.

You could have emotion-fuelled argu- ments back and forth about who's more selfish: the couple who wants the perfect nuclear family and follows biological, social and moral imperatives, or the one who steps off the commuter belt.

Then we could get into the murky territory about preserving race—it's certain groups that are breeding: immigrants, the poor and uneducated. There are more children where women have less freedom. That should drive us to bring more freedom to those countries, or areas, or Australian cultures. While understanding that it's ever been thus, the recipe that makes up the rich broth of the gene pool is a moving feast. But, again, we need to think about how that works out, why and whether or not it's necessary to do anything about it.

The chaotic cacophony of choice has led to a situation we're not prepared for, or talking about enough. Both individually and at a policy level. The norm is changing; we're becoming more childless. While another norm is sustained: thinking of the childless as aberrant.

This issue is already a breeding ground for bitter comparisons and brutal accusations, which is both paralysing and saddening because it should be about love—and Australia recently overwhelmingly agreed that love is love, in whatever form it takes.

Freedom over ourselves and our reproductive capacity and choices is in every way marvellous, and still new; so we'll be navigating these treacherous (sometimes broken) waters for a long time to come. Meanwhile, despite hifalutin talk about pronatalist government policies, feminist fury and frustrated freedoms, women are just getting on with their own personal (oh-god-I-hate-this-word) journeys. Brewing their own identities even as this world tries to thrust its own upon them.

A reminder popped up on my Facebook feed not so long ago. It was a post from a trip I did with one of my favourite people in the world, Sarah Martin. Journo, singer, sewer, friend. We'd gone on a trip with pre-ousted prime minister Malcolm Turnbull. One of those trips that you suspect people cock a disbelieving eyebrow at when you recount the tale at dinner parties. We toured the scene of the London Bridge attack with Theresa May, and went to the Champs-Élysées to see Emmanuel and Brigitte Macron (where the press room springs for charcuterie, cheese and wine). She saw the Queen. I was doing something else at the time, I can't remember what.

The highlight was the G20 summit in Hamburg. Trump was there in his souped-up car; everyone was there. Including anti-capitalist rioters who attacked police, set cars on fire and shouted 'Welcome to Hell' as they were tear-gassed. We had a cracker of a night. We'd been told to definitely, absolutely under-no-circumstances go to the riots in the Reeperbahn district. People had been working themselves up for weeks over the world leaders' arrival in the town. Don't go there. So we did. Dodged Molotov cocktails, watched streams of riot police march through, posed with anti-riot cars. Drank dodgy wine while wandering the streets. Saw a sign to a sex worker area that said 'No women'. Went there. Risked gonorrhoea of the eyeball. That's a story for another day. Eventually we toddled back from the red light district to our hotel. It was around 2 a.m.

The red carpet was out, as was the Russian flag. Even our Gewurztraminer-soaked minds worked out what that meant. We were about to run into Putin. We almost did. We saw him, tried to pap him. His goons put their meaty hands all over our stuff. I remember Sarah giving them a serve about freedom of the press, then security was called and eventually it was a proper international diplomatic incident.

So I texted her on the anniversary, when FB reminded me, about that time we tried to pap Putin, got gooned, created an international incident. She texted back a leisurely couple of hours later. She was making felt platypi for a mobile for her new baby, Frankie.

'Same, same,' she said. 'This is pretty wild, too.'

I chortled, then had an unexpected feeling of calm. It was like the eye in the hurricane of FOMO and competition and judging each other on our dinner party stories and our tick-the-box achievements. My stupid smart mate was still having adventures, just different ones.

Which is how it mostly is, and always should be. Canberra—and Washington—will fiddle around the edges but they won't change anything fundamental for us, anytime soon. Women—and men—can fight for change but in the meantime hope to shift between work and life and play without being judged. Different lives, same people, complex identities. That's freedom: individual freedom.

Acknowledgements

For Mum and Dad, who made me, then made me read. And Sarah Martin, who made me write this.

As for Louise Adler (who probably had bigger things on her mind) and Sally Heath (who took the edge off my imposter syndrome)—I've already used up all my words. Thank you.

And to Matt Gilbertson, AKA the Boy Wonder from Berlin, because he asked, and now he owes me.